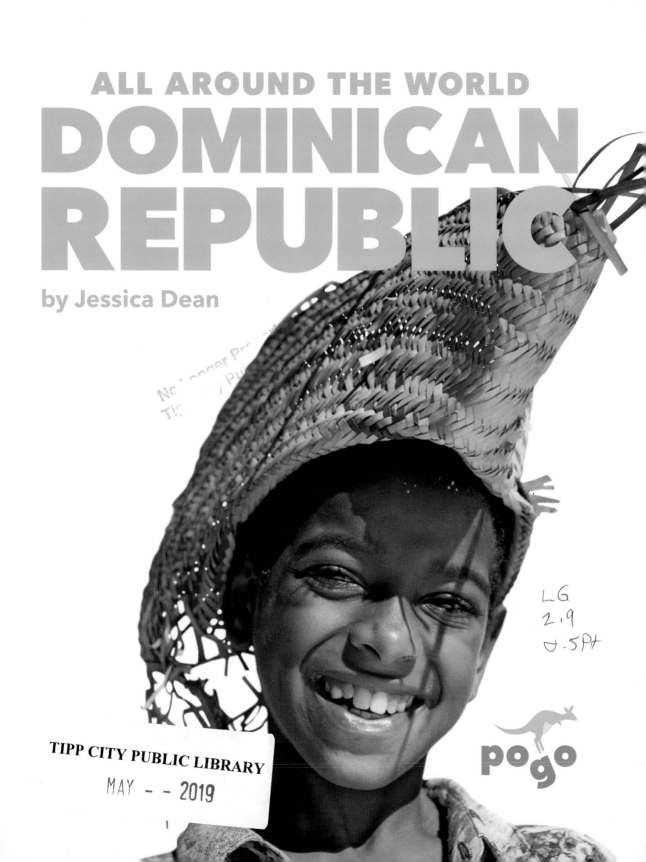

ALL AROUND THE WORLD
DOMINICAN REPUBLIC

by Jessica Dean

pogo

Ideas for Parents and Teachers

Pogo Books let children practice reading informational text while introducing them to nonfiction features such as headings, labels, sidebars, maps, and diagrams, as well as a table of contents, glossary, and index.

Carefully leveled text with a strong photo match offers early fluent readers the support they need to succeed.

Before Reading

• "Walk" through the book and point out the various nonfiction features. Ask the student what purpose each feature serves.

• Look at the glossary together. Read and discuss the words.

Read the Book

• Have the child read the book independently.

• Invite him or her to list questions that arise from reading.

After Reading

• Discuss the child's questions. Talk about how he or she might find answers to those questions.

• Prompt the child to think more. Ask: The Dominican Republic celebrates independence with parades and costumes. Do you celebrate Independence Day where you live? How do you celebrate it?

Pogo Books are published by Jump!
5357 Penn Avenue South
Minneapolis, MN 55419
www.jumplibrary.com

Library of Congress Cataloging-in-Publication Data

Names: Dean, Jessica, 1963-
Title: Dominican Republic : all around the world / Jessica Dean. | Description: Minneapolis, MN: Jump!, Inc., 2019. | Series: All around the world "Pogo Books." | Includes index.
Identifiers: LCCN 2018020125 (print)
LCCN 2018020700 (ebook)
ISBN 9781641281454 (ebook)
ISBN 9781641281430 (hardcover : alk. paper)
ISBN 9781641281447 (pbk.)
Subjects: LCSH: Dominican Republic–Juvenile literature.
Classification: LCC F1934.2 (ebook)
LCC F1934.2 .D33 2019 (print) | DDC 972.93–dc23
LC record available at https://lccn.loc.gov/2018020125

Editor: Kristine Spanier
Designer: Molly Ballanger

Photo Credits: saaton/Shutterstock, cover; Buena Vista Images/Getty, 1; Pixfiction/Shutterstock, 3; Ger Bosma/Alamy, 4; 1Photodiva/Getty, 5; Zaneta Cichawa/Shutterstock, 6-7; Ivan Godal/Shutterstock, 8-9tl; cinoby/iStock, 8-9tr; clark42/iStock, 8-9bl; 33karen33/iStock, 8-9br; Valentin Valkov/Shutterstock, 10; Luis Davilla/Getty, 11; orava/iStock, 12-13; KIKE CALVO/Alamy, 14-15; Anamaria Mejia/Shutterstock, 16; Rainer Hackenberg/Alamy, 17; Roberto Machado Noa/Getty, 18-19; GeorgiaFlash/Alamy, 20-21; Robert Hackett/Shutterstock, 23.

Printed in the United States of America at Corporate Graphics in North Mankato, Minnesota.

TABLE OF CONTENTS

CHAPTER 1

WELCOME TO THE DOMINICAN REPUBLIC!

Marvel at a rare iguana. Visit a Spanish **fort**. Enjoy fresh fruit on a warm beach. Welcome to the Dominican Republic!

rhinoceros iguana

pictograph

This country shares an island with Haiti. It is in the Caribbean Sea. Deep caves on the coast are covered in **pictographs**. They are more than 600 years old. **Indigenous** people who once called the island home made them.

Explore hidden rooms at this old Spanish fort. It was built in 1502. People here once used it to defend the country. Against who? The British and French. It was also used to protect the land from pirates. They wanted the island's gold.

Fortaleza Ozama

pelican

sea turtle

alligator

manatee

Tropical weather here is cooled by ocean breezes. **Hurricanes** are a threat in the spring and fall.

Swamps are home to flamingos, pelicans, and alligators. Dolphins, sea turtles, and manatees swim near the coast.

DID YOU KNOW?

Every winter, 3,000 to 5,000 humpback whales arrive here. Why? To give birth in the warm waters.

CHAPTER 2

LIFE IN THE DOMINICAN

Many people travel here to spend time on the beautiful beaches. **Tourism** is a great source of **revenue** for the country.

Santo Domingo is one of the oldest cities in the Caribbean. Between 1655 and 1864, different governments struggled for control of the city. Where were they from? Spain. France. Haiti.

Santo Domingo

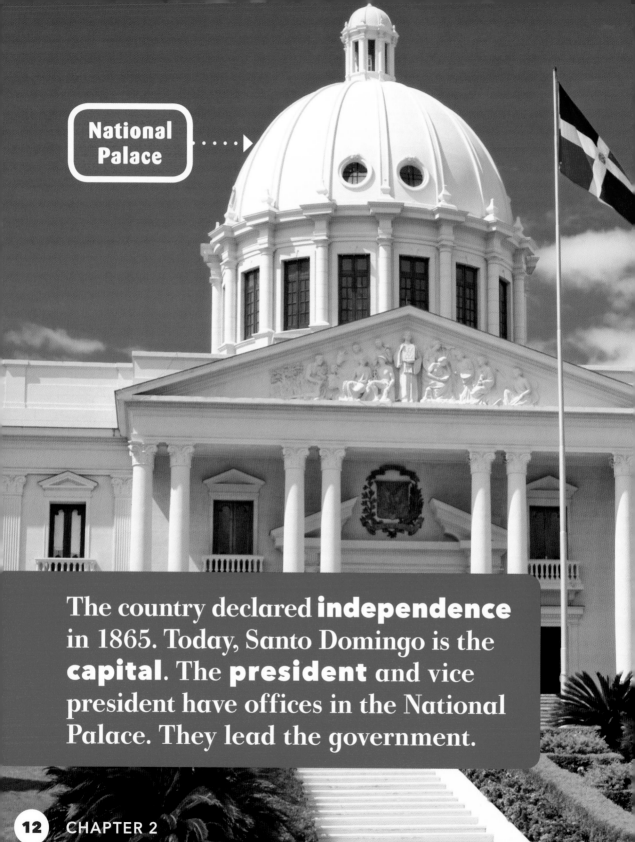

National Palace

The country declared **independence** in 1865. Today, Santo Domingo is the **capital**. The **president** and vice president have offices in the National Palace. They lead the government.

TAKE A LOOK!

Take a look at the country flag. It shows the Bible open to a **verse** about freedom. Every element of the flag has special meaning to its people.

■ = progress and liberty
■ = people who fought for freedom
□ = peace and faith

1 laurel branch: immortality
2 palm branch: liberty
3 Bible verse: "And the truth shall make you free."

Children begin school at the age of six. Many students leave after eighth grade. Why? They may not have enough money for school supplies or books. Or the students might need to work on family farms. Or help take care of younger siblings.

WHAT DO YOU THINK?

Some students finish high school. Do you think students should leave school early to help out at home? Or is it better to get more education?

CHAPTER 3

FOOD, FUN, AND CELEBRATIONS

Most food is grown on the island. Breakfast is sweet bread or mashed plantains. These are like bananas. The big meal is lunch. Beans and rice are popular. They may be served with chicken and salad.

plantain

Farms here grow coffee or cacao beans. Others grow sugarcane or rice. Fruit grows throughout the country. Like what? Papaya. Passion fruit. Grapefruit. Many **crops** are **exported**.

cacao ·····▶

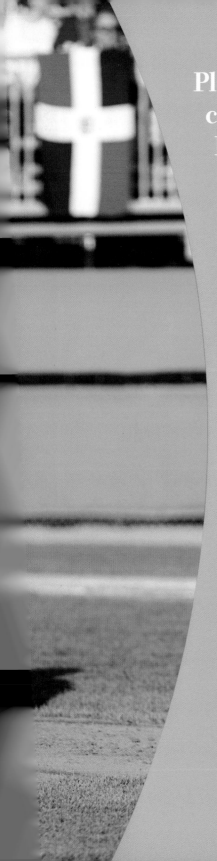

Play ball! Baseball is the country's favorite sport. Fans cheer for their teams.

Another popular game is dominoes. Tables are set up in parks and outside of shops.

WHAT DO YOU THINK?

Kids learn dominoes from their families. Does your family have a game that everyone plays together?

Holidays here are full of fun. Carnival celebrates the Easter season. People enjoy taking part in the parades, costumes, and music. The biggest parade celebrates independence on February 27 each year.

This is a pretty country. Would you like to visit?

QUICK FACTS & TOOLS

DOMINICAN REPUBLIC

Location: Caribbean Sea

Size: 18,792 square miles
(48,670 square kilometers)

Population: 10,734,247
(July 2017 estimate)

Capital: Santo Domingo

Type of Government:
presidential republic

Language: Spanish

Exports: gold, silver, cocoa,
sugar, coffee

Currency: Dominican peso

capital: A city where government leaders meet.

crops: Plants grown for food.

exported: Sold to other countries.

fort: A place that is fortified against attack.

hurricanes: Violent storms with heavy rain and high winds.

independence: Freedom from a controlling authority.

indigenous: Living or existing naturally in a particular region or environment.

pictographs: Pictures used as symbols in ancient writing.

president: The leader of a country.

revenue: Income produced by a given source.

tourism: The business of serving people who are traveling for pleasure.

verse: A section from the Bible.

Dominican Republic's currency

INDEX

TO LEARN MORE

Learning more is as easy as 1, 2, 3.

1) Go to www.factsurfer.com

2) Enter "DominicanRepublic" into the search box.

3) Click the "Surf" button to see a list of websites.

With factsurfer, finding more information is just a click away.